## About the Author

The author is a grandfather, currently working for the frontline NHS.

He is a retired police officer.

He enjoys football and is an active referee and mentor.

He has enjoyed a long working life in public service and engagement in community voluntary activities.

He likes walking, genealogy, amateur photography and writing poetry.

**Dedications**

This work is dedicated to my grandchildren, Shaun James Thompson Daulby and Chloe Louise Thompson.

They inspired this project with their enthusiasm and interest in dinosaurs during our many visits to the attraction.

James GR Thompson

# SHAUN AND THE DINOSAURS

Austin Macauley Publishers™

LONDON · CAMBRIDGE · NEW YORK · SHARJAH

Copyright © James GR Thompson 2021

The right of James GR Thompson to be identified as author of this work has been asserted by the author in accordance with section 77 and 78 of the Copyright, Designs and Patents Act 1988.

All rights reserved. No part of this publication may be reproduced, stored in a retrieval system, or transmitted in any form or by any means, electronic, mechanical, photocopying, recording, or otherwise, without the prior permission of the publishers.

Any person who commits any unauthorised act in relation to this publication may be liable to criminal prosecution and civil claims for damages.

A CIP catalogue record for this title is available from the British Library.

ISBN 9781398438484 (Paperback)
ISBN 9781398438491 (ePub e-book)

www.austinmacauley.com

First Published 2021
Austin Macauley Publishers Ltd
1 Canada Square
Canary Wharf
London
E14 5AA

# Chapter 1

Shaun lived with his parents and little sister, Chloe, whom he called 'Co – Co'. Chloe could not yet speak properly but she was clever and understood everyone.

Shaun was bright and most adventurous. He liked to learn how things worked. He always asked questions of the grown-ups. He worked well with his classmates and had many friends.

Shaun loved animals. He adored his dog, Tassie, and his Granddad's cats. He appreciated wild animals like crocodiles, lizards and snakes.

But his greatest love was dinosaurs. Shaun collected models of them that became friends and he took them everywhere. He gave them names. There was Tyrone the Tyrannosaurus Rex; Valerie the Velociraptor; Peter the Plesiosaur; Steve the Stegosaurus; Tricia the Triceratops; David the Diplodocus. There was Trevor the Pterodactyl, Anna the Allosaurus, Stanley the Styracosaurus; the twins, Paul and Pamela the Pachycephalasauruses, Imelda the Iguanodon, and Amy the Abelisaurus.

At bedtime, Shaun often dreamt of great adventures with his dinosaur friends.

## Chapter 2

One fine day, Shaun went to the seaside with his family. He ambled along the beach when suddenly, he saw ripples in the rock pools. As he peered into the clear water, he saw baby crabs stranded at the bottom. He knew that the seagulls might find them. He picked them up gently and he put some of the water into his bucket to protect them. He went to the shore and placed them carefully into the sea and watched anxiously as they crawled furiously towards deeper water. He smiled and returned to his sister.

They played for a while. Chloe yawned. And her Mum put her into her buggy. Soon, Chloe snoozed contentedly. Shaun too was tired. He lay down on his towel on the soft sand and drifted off.

Granddad gently picked Shaun up. He placed him in his seat in the car.

# Chapter 3

Shaun began to dream vividly. They were driving to Dinosaur Park for the first time. They drove past the mountains, the deep blue sea and the old castle on the mountainside. They drove into the park where Grandad stopped. They reached the Dinosaur Park. As they entered, a huge Tyrannosaurus, like Shaun's model stood out. The monster stood with eyes blazing and jaws open wide baring his pointed teeth. His claws sprawled out in front, menacingly. The children were anxious.

Shaun wondered: "If he was real, I could talk to him. He looks mean, but I can't show him that I'm scared." An idea struck him. "I'll say 'hello.' I'm not chicken."

He breathed deeply and said fearlessly, "Hello, Mr Dinosaur."

Suddenly, the dinosaur turned his head and looked down. His eyes widened and he smiled. "Hello Shaun," he replied softly.

Shaun was astounded. "How do you know who I am?" he spluttered.

The dinosaur tittered, "Your name's on your 'T' shirt."

Shaun nodded. "I suppose you know my sister's name?"

"It's Chloe," the dinosaur laughed. "She's got her name on too."

"Well, who are *these* people?" declared Shaun defiantly.

"Mum and Grandpa Jim," Tyrone replied teasingly. He had guessed this from overhearing them talking.

Shaun shook his head. "What's your name?"

"Tyrone," the dinosaur replied.

"What?" said Shaun.

Shaun was incredulous. He looked at Mum and Granddad who saw nothing. Chloe waved at the dinosaur.

"Hello, Chloe," said Tyrone. "Nakka, di yappa doo-ee," Chloe shrieked, delighted.

"I don't understand," said Shaun quizzically. "Why can't Mum and Granddad see you?"

"Aha!" said Tyrone, tapping his enormous snout, "It's magic. Only children can see me. The grown-ups don't believe in magic, so they only see a still model, not the real me."

Shaun looked around. Mum and Granddad were unaware that Tyrone was alive.

"But the grown-ups will soon realise," said Shaun doubtfully.

"No, they won't Shaun," laughed Tyrone. "We are invisible to them. Only children can see us. That's their special privilege."

"I can't believe this," said Shaun, his heart pounding. "I talk to my models, but they can't speak."

"When you talk to them, we can hear you. We know how you feel sometimes," said Tyrone.

Shaun had a million questions for his new friend. He looked anxiously at the adults. Tyrone continued, "Because the magic is powerful, it copies all of us, you and Chloe too, to deceive them. It worked when you said 'hello.'"

Shaun stammered, "Look, Chloe, they're all standing there with us looking at Tyrone who isn't moving. This is magic!"

Tyrone was pulling tongues at Chloe who roared with delight.

"Tyrone," Shaun said seriously, "Isn't T-Rex fierce?"

Tyrone looked at the little boy's quizzical face.

"We used to be when there were only dinosaurs around," he replied. "We had to fight other dinosaurs to live but that changed."

"What happened?" Shaun asked him intrigued.

"One day, it went dark. We all fell asleep. I woke up and saw the other dinosaurs that live here. No-one knew how we got here."

"I was told that the dinosaurs died out millions of years ago. We know about you because they found bones in the ground."

"That's right Shaun" replied Tyrone.

"Tyrone, I don't understand. How did you all come alive again?"

"One day, a great wizard came over the mountains. He told us we were very special and that we had been saved to do special deeds," Tyrone answered.

Shaun and Chloe listened intently to the dinosaur's story.

Tyrone continued. "The magician told us some humans would fall into danger and might need special help. He told us that we would help when they needed it most. Good children would help too."

Shaun blushed. He and Chloe were naughty sometimes and Mummy had to chide them.

Tyrone smiled. "Humans aren't perfect. They misbehave, especially children. If you care about others, you are a good person."

Shaun whistled with relief. Chloe gave Tyrone a beaming smile and the great dinosaur grinned back.

"If you two weren't really good I couldn't talk to you," he said chirpily.

"Tyrone, you're not going to eat us if we're wicked are you?" Shaun asked cheekily.

The dinosaur cackled, "Of course not! I'd rather have pizza with chocolate chip ice cream for afters!"

Shaun chuckled.

"Listen," Tyrone said changing the subject. 'Would you two like to meet the gang?'

"Oh yes," said Shaun enthusiastically. Chloe clapped her hands in delight.

"Let's go then," said Tyrone jovially. "Don't worry the grown-ups won't suspect a thing!"

Tyrone unbuckled the safety belt on Chloe's pushchair. He took her hand gently in one claw and took Shaun's in the other.

"Let's meet the twins," suggested Tyrone.

"Okay with me," replied Shaun confidently.

"Ba – oo – nee – nee badda," replied Chloe joyfully.

"I guess she agrees," laughed Tyrone.

# Chapter 4

The trio walked slowly towards the Pachycephalasauruses, Paul and Pamela who were playfully banging heads together.

"Hey, stop for a moment," shouted Tyrone. "Come and meet my new pals!" The twins looked up in surprise.

"Hello," said Shaun politely. "I'm Shaun and this is my little sister Chloe."

"Delighted to meet you," replied the twins together.

"They want to be friends," Tyrone replied.

"Of course," said the twins.

"Doesn't it hurt when you bang your heads together?" Shaun asked.

The twins laughed. "We're too thick-headed to feel the pain," they joked.

"Let's see the others," Tyrone interrupted, "They'll all be dying to meet you.'

The little troupe set off again. Shaun looked back nervously towards the adults but as Tyrone promised, the magic fooled them. Chloe cackled joyfully as she held Tyrone's gentle claw. Shaun felt more reassured as they ambled along.

At the next enclosure, he stopped in awe. Here stood the largest creature he had ever seen, taller than a house. He craned his neck to find the monster's head.

Tyrone grinned. He whistled loudly and a long neck dropped swiftly like a waterfall. A small head appeared and stopped short of the ground.

Chloe's eyes opened wide. She held her breath. Shaun's jaw dropped, as the head turned towards them. Two gentle eyes fluttered dozily and a deep, slow voice exclaimed, Hello children. I'm David."

Shaun was astounded. This Diplodocus was huge. Chloe adored David's docile smile and she gurgled approvingly.

Tyrone spoke, "He is a gentle giant. He looks frightening but he's a big softie. He adores children. We call him 'Dozy' because he always looks sleepy but when you need him, he's always there."

David grinned. "Would you like a sweet, children?" he asked.

"Yes please," Shaun answered politely, "But where are they?"

"Look around my neck," David continued, "Do you see the little pouch on the necklace? I have a few jellybeans left. Take one for Chloe too."

Shaun gripped the pouch and fished inside. He gave his little sister a bright red sweet and he took an orange one.

"Thank you, this tastes nice," he replied gratefully.

"My pleasure," drawled David in his deep, low tone.

"Come," Tyrone directed, "There are more of us to meet."

# Chapter 5

The group continued. As they turned past a tall bush, Valerie the Velociraptor leapt into view and stopped in front of them. She placed her sharp jaws immediately in front of Chloe's little face and snarled.

Chloe began to tremble. Shaun stood bravely in front of her and declared, "I'll punch you on the nose if you hurt my little sister!"

Valerie halted. She replied, "I won't. I was testing you. I know you would protect other people. I'm sorry I frightened you, Chloe." Chloe responded with a wide grin.

Everyone chortled and the growing band of friends wandered off to meet more allies. They walked to the edge of the Park. There they met Steve, the Stegosaurus, scratching the large spines on his back against a tree trunk.

"Ooh this heat!" he exclaimed painfully.

Tyrone called, "Come and meet the children."

"This is Shaun and Chloe," Valerie chirped, "They're our special guests."

"You couldn't scratch my spines, could you?" Steve pleaded, "I can't reach."

"All right," Shaun volunteered, "I see that you're having trouble."

Tyrone lifted Shaun and Chloe onto Steve's back where they rubbed his spines vigorously. Steve sighed blissfully.

"Shall we meet the rest?" Tyrone suggested.

"Smashing," Shaun replied enthusiastically.

"This will save time."

Tyrone raised his claw to his mouth. To Shaun's astonishment, he blew silently on a silver whistle. Shaun mused. "I wish Chloe and I could have one like that!"

# Chapter 6

New arrivals answered Tyrone's magical whistle. Shaun stood agog when he saw the dinosaurs before him and his sister. Tricia the Triceratops nodded. Trevor the Pterodactyl somersaulted. Anna the Allosaurus winked. Stanley the Styracosaurus waved, Imelda the Iguanodon bowed, and Amy, the Abelisaurus smiled.

Seconds later, Peter the Plesiosaur squelched into view.

"Everyone, meet our new friends Shaun and Chloe," Tyrone announced.

The dinosaurs cheered. Shaun was astounded. Real creatures stood before him like they must have been when they roamed the Earth and moved freely in the clean air and the only sounds were theirs. He couldn't imagine the Earth being so old.

The dinosaurs jostled to speak to the children. Chloe cooed with glee.

"Tyrone, have you ever done anything amazing yet?" Shaun enquired.

"We've found lost children before, but we've not done anything brave or exciting."

Shaun replied, "My Granddad says, we all have our moments and I'm sure yours will come."

Shaun had a million questions to ask. Tyrone knew his pal was curious. He knew how to help him. "Ask us, in turn, to tell you about ourselves," he suggested. "Let's get some lemonade first. I'm thirsty."

Shaun looked at him quizzically. "How can you buy a lemonade; do you have money?"

"No, magic," smiled Tyrone, tapping his snout. "The Wizard gives us our treats. We wish for them and they appear."

## Chapter 7

The friends ambled into the shop. The serving ladies carried on regardless. To Shaun's surprise, there was a tray of cool drinks waiting on the counter.

"Come on," Tyrone announced, "The Magician has read our thoughts!" Everyone drank heartily.

Tyrone sat on the edge of a table and invited the children to ask the dinosaurs questions about themselves. Then, a radio crackled, as two policemen arrived. One officer stopped and listened. The other asked for two refreshing glasses of lemonade.

Shaun and Chloe watched them closely. Granddad was a policeman too. The smiley officer chatted with the ladies, as the drinks were poured. His friend shook his head slowly.

"What's up, Bob?" his pal enquired gently.

Bob replied, "There's a fire at the Children's' Hospital – people may be trapped. There's a roadblock stopping help getting through."

The ladies gasped. Bob looked shaken and Barry his colleague, announced, "We've got to go."

The two policemen dashed into the car park and sped off in their patrol car.

"Oh my word," whispered Tyrone. "Those poor children. What can we do?"

Shaun whispered to Tyrone. "Why don't we go too? Didn't you say that you had special powers to help people in need?"

Tyrone scratched his head nervously. "We've never had to do anything big before."

"Neither have we," replied Shaun.

Tyrone looked at the other dinosaurs. They saw him as their leader. He must decide what to do. His claws trembled. Shaun saw this. "I'm worried too, but we've got to do something," he said softly.

"You're right. We have magic on our side!" The big Dinosaur gave a toothy grin and everyone cheered. "I may be big and strong, Shaun, but I'm terrified," Tyrone confided.

"So am I," Shaun announced quietly. "I only hope we can get there in time..."

"Does anyone know the way?" asked Anna suddenly. No one replied.

Trevor fidgeted and Chloe waddled over to him.

"Ee ha doo, baddy gaga moke," she uttered in her baby talk.

Trevor nodded his head. Shaun realised that they had a plan.

"What is it, Co-Co?" he enquired.

She whispered in his ear. Shaun announced, "She's right, Trevor can fly over the town and see what's going on and report back."

A cheer rang out. This seemed a sensible solution, but Shaun halted.

"What's wrong," Tyrone queried anxiously.

"Trevor might find the hospital but we have to get into town. We will have to fight our way through the traffic." Everyone looked glum. What could they do now?

# Chapter 8

Shaun and Tyrone had done most of the thinking, but as they wracked their brains for ideas, Chloe and Trevor chatted secretly in the corner of the room. Chloe chortled, as Trevor shrieked gleefully.

Tyrone turned angrily. "This is no time for merry-making. This is serious. The children are in danger."

Shaun was surprised that his sister joked at such a dangerous time. She waved him over and whispered in his ear.

"Tyrone, these two are marvels," roared Shaun joyfully. "They've got a great idea."

"Let's hear it quickly," Tyrone beamed, "We must act soon."

"Well, Chloe will ride on Trevor's back, like a pilot and she can tell us what going on from above. We can team up to direct operations."

"Very good," said Tyrone, "But how can we talk to each other? We have our whistles, but how can we speak?"

"No problem," laughed Shaun. "Mum and Granddad have mobile phones. We know how to use them. If Chloe takes one and I take the other, we can pass on information."

Tyrone's eyes widened. "I get it; it's like having an army or an air force helping each other."

"That's right," Shaun reassured. "Chloe and Trevor can get to the scene quickly and tell us what's going on and where we need to go. You and I, the ground commanders, can direct everyone else. We can use the whistles if we need to."

The dinosaurs cheered together. It was a wonderful solution. The group saw Tyrone as their leader and would do whatever he asked of them. Trevor was delighted to assist. As he could fly, he could do important work on this occasion.

"We need to make sure Chloe's safe on Trevor's back," Anna advised wisely.

Shaun nodded. "Yes, we can use her buggy harness and some of that strong rope that's outside by the groundsman's hut."

The excited group rushed outside and gathered the pieces necessary to ensure Chloe's safety. Shaun dashed straight to Mum and Granddad. He wondered how he could take the phones without their knowledge. He remembered the magic. If it worked, he could sneak in and they would suspect nothing. He knew the phones were in their jacket pockets. If he took them gently, he would succeed.

He approached them cautiously. He took his Mum's first then Granddad's. They suspected nothing. He swiftly rejoined the group.

When he returned, the dinosaurs had Chloe ready. Imelda and Anna had nimbly tied the ropes to her harness and strapped her securely onto Trevor's back. Trevor waited patiently for his instructions. He was beaming with enthusiasm for the task ahead.

Shaun looked at Tyrone and the pair looked around the others.

"Are we ready?" Shaun asked nervously.

"All for one another," drawled David wisely. Everyone else nodded his or her heads in turn.

Tyrone looked serious. "We've got to move quickly and together," he added slowly.

"We need a plan," Shaun quipped. "What if Chloe and Trevor get up into the air and we follow them? We can sort out who does what when we get there."

"Great. Let's move," Tyrone added.

Everyone leapt forward and they rushed outside into the car park. A whooshing sound arose and in seconds, Trevor flew up above them. Chloe chortled as the wind rushed through her hair. She gripped the mobile phone tightly in one hand and with the other, she held the reins.

Shaun looked at Tyrone.

"Jump up on my shoulders and hang onto to the chain on my neck if that helps," Tyrone suggested.

"I think I'll use rope too, just to be safe." Shaun replied as he removed the piece of rope from his waist that he had thoughtfully gathered before he had re-joined the group.

"Are we ready?" Shaun queried sensibly. "It might help us all to bring along some of that rope. You never know!"

"We'll take some around our necks," answered the twins as one.

"I'll take some too," added Imelda.

"Me too," Anna joined in.

"Good," roared Tyrone. "Have we all got our whistles? We may get split up later on and we'll need to stay in touch."

The eager group checked their necks and once assured that each has his or precious whistle dangling, they were ready.

"We must go now," Shaun shouted confidently.

The heroes looked at each other. Everyone was nervous, as each gave a wry smile and nodded.

"Just a small detail," Peter asked timidly. "With my flippers, I won't be able to race along with you."

David spoke up. "Wiggle yourself along my tail and jump onto my back. I'm the heavyweight around here so I'll be the slowest. We'll get there together!"

Peter flipped and flopped along the floor and quickly crawled onto David's back.

"Hold tight and we're off," David shouted boldly.

The group nodded to one another and sprang into action.

"Let's do it," they roared and they charged off across the car park.

# Chapter 9

The friends rushed outside the Dinosaur Park into the public grounds. They looked around in the brilliant sunlight at the little family groups playing happily on the grass. Everyone halted, took a deep breath and prepared for the great task ahead.

Chloe was bristling with excitement. "Nannu – ki – apply – dagu," she exclaimed, as they waited hovered over the main park.

"Come on gang, it's now or never," Shaun rallied.

With that command, he gripped tightly to the rope around Tyrone's neck and held the mobile phone ready to speak with Chloe. She nodded to her brother, whispered in Trevor's ear. He darted upwards, as Chloe shrieked with the warm summer air rushing over her face.

The dinosaurs followed Tyrone, as he charged towards the gates of the public park.

Chloe and Trevor soon hovered high overhead and kept the ground force in view. Shaun suddenly thought to test the mobiles phones. He dialled Chloe's phone and the little girl answered immediately.

"Can you hear me okay Co-Co?" he enquired.

"Noona – peegu – nibby," she replied. Shaun knew that she was ready for action.

The group reached the gate and looked for signs to lead them into town. Shaun remembered that as Granddad drove to the park, they had passed the sea and there was a big brown sign pointing to the Town Centre.

"I think we should follow that road alongside the sea. I guess the town will be very busy if we go the other way. Do you remember the policemen's radios? They said that there was a huge traffic jam. We need to miss that!"

"Good thinking partner," Tyrone nodded. "I think they call that the Promenade."

The group turned and promptly reached the coast where they saw the sign that Shaun reported. They dashed off along the wide pavement. It was busy, but the pavement was so wide that they could slip past the pedestrians easily. Above them, Chloe and Trevor flew steadily towards the town centre. Shaun's phone rang. He answered and Chloe reported.

"Doogu – peeka – hee- oo – kokku – danta."

"Chloe says they can see flames in the distance," he advised. Tyrone nodded, knowing they were on the correct course.

The group ran effortlessly, passing street after street. They were running strongly yet wondered why they were not tiring. The magic must have given them super energy!

They ran mightily as Chloe and Trevor kept up the lead in the air. The ground force followed them dutifully, as they glided towards the scene. The sky was clear and the Promenade had few hazards.

Chloe saw flames in the sky and told Trevor. He tilted his beak and sped up. He rose higher and faster. Shaun noticed this and prompted Tyrone.

"We must be and there must be a danger. Look they're racing off towards it."

Tyrone nodded. "Hurry it up, gang. It must be really serious," he added dolefully.

The group met some congestion at the end of the Promenade. The fire had caused chaos in town and the traffic had backed up considerably. This was causing major problems for the emergency services making to the scene.

They reached the start of the tail-back and Shaun saw Trevor hovering and Chloe waving to them.

"They must be close to the hospital. They are working out what to do," he said.

His phone rang. Chloe reported eagerly.

"Pippi – oocka – lalab – ee –dinku!" she chattered hurriedly.

"Yes," Shaun replied to the group, "They're right over it now."

Tyrone looked on hard. David raised his head as high as he could.

"I can see the roof of the hospital straight ahead," he drawled, "There's fire coming from the side. I can see people on the roof."

The others looked around for the quickest route. Cars littered the road. People stood around trying to see what the crisis. People stood about aimlessly, scratching their heads. Drivers angrily sounded their horns, but nothing could move. It was a total jam.

David looked around for any side routes but there was no other way to approach the hospital.

"This is a fix," Shaun uttered angrily.

The dinosaurs nodded sadly. Steve, who had had little to say, had an idea.

"Listen, we're heavyweights. Let's use force to shift these cars. As long as we don't hurt the people, we should get a path through this lot."

"Of course," added Tricia, "We should put our size to good use!"

The group agreed. On all sides were parked cars and vans and people gazing curiously at the road ahead.

"Come on guys," said Tyrone, "Let's put our backs into it."

David led, leaning firmly onto a parked lorry. It slowly moved sideways under his great weight. Tricia followed and pushed her body into a small motorcar into the gutter. Tyrone weighed in and shoved aside a motorcycle.

The others followed pushed cars aside. The smaller dinosaurs joined in and soon, they made a wide berth for them to pass.

"This will help the fire engines to get through," Shaun announced triumphantly.

"Yes, I wondered how they'd do it," Tyrone replied, "I think we've solved the problem!"

The twins who were ahead stopped behind a huge crowd of onlookers. David wallowed up behind and peered over the last line to see how deep the ranks were.

"I can't tell how many people there are. There are so many standing so deep. We'll never get through!"

Shaun rubbed his chin. He looked towards Chloe and Trevor hovering above them. Chloe waved and pointed. Shaun realised she was indicating where the danger was, so they had to act smartly.

Shaun cried out, "Let's not mess around. The children are in real danger. These grown-ups are a nuisance and we have to shift them. The children can't suffer," he added resolutely.

"I agree," said Tyrone. "Come on everyone, backs into it. Let's do it."

The dinosaurs breathed and pushed into the people nearest to them. David leant gently and sent over a hundred people tumbling like skittles. No one was hurt. As they got to their feet, they looked bewildered; did a freak gust of wind strike them?

Valerie tried to shove a huge man, but she was too weak. She started to get frustrated and began to curse him. He turned around to look at who was pushing him and he was surprised to see the smaller dinosaur facing him. For a second, he thought it was a person wearing a costume and he laughed at her.

"Ho, ho, fancy dress, eh?" He sniggered.

Valerie became angry. "You think this is funny? Try this!" She stooped and nibbled at his ankle with her sharp teeth. He jumped back in shock and gave her passage at once.

Tyrone saw what had happened. "That man shouldn't have seen you, Valerie, perhaps the magic is wearing off?"

Valerie closed her eyes and thought for a moment.

"No, it's probably because I was angry before I nipped him. I know what should have happened. Provided we keep calm, the magic should keep us invisible. The minute we let anger take over, we lose our cover. I should clear my head and stop being nasty," she replied humbly.

The group looked around. There were still too many people around to let them through. They could hear sirens in the distance and that must have been the fire engines trying to make to the scene. However, the noise did not grow any louder and this meant that the machines could not get through the traffic.

# Chapter 10

Tyrone groaned. The hard work so far looked in vain. The cars and vans had been moved aside to the emergency vehicles to get through but only so far. There was still some way to go...

Chloe waved at Shaun frantically and his mobile phone rang. He listened intently and frowned.

"Guys, this is serious. The roof's burning and there are children on it." He scratched his head. "We must get mean with this, people. They are not helping to stand around. We'll have to shift them with more force."

"Let's scare them if we have to," Anna shrieked.

"Yes!" everyone shouted together.

The friends turned towards the crowd. They formed two lines alongside each other. Tyrone took his position at the head to them forwards. He looked at everyone. "Have you all still got your whistles?"

Everyone nodded.

"You bigger ones, stay on the left side because most of the crowd is there. Your weight should shift them easily. The lighter ones go on the right. There are fewer people there," Tyrone directed. "Right, let's mean business," he added grimly. "If they see us, too bad."

"Yes," Shaun added, "But who would believe them if they said they had been attacked by a crowd of dinosaurs with two children helping them?"

Everyone chortled.

"That would be great fun," added Valerie mischievously, as she clattered her teeth together.

"But no hurting anyone," Tyrone warned. "Don't forget, we're here to help people."

The troupe lined up like a platoon of soldiers. Shaun and Tyrone stood in the command position. Chloe and Trevor remained high overhead waiting for instructions.

Shaun looked around. Every second was now vital. There were no fire engines in view. The crowd murmured, realising the situation. Panic might break out now.

"We must make sure no-one else gets involved because they might get in our way," he announced wisely.

"Right, let's go, on three," yelled Tyrone.

Shaun turned to his mobile phone and rang Chloe.

"Leave the phone on, CoCo. We must keep talking so we miss nothing."

"Ooky – mabba – piggu – laaka," Chloe replied.

"Okay, here's the count," said Shaun firmly. "One – Two – Threeee!"

The group moved off sharply. They moved forward and pushed outwards into the crowd. The first rows of people moved slowly apart. As the dinosaurs kept control of their emotions, no – one saw them yet. Several people got to their feet and looked around quizzically trying to work out what had knocked them over. Someone shouted, "Did you feel that wind? Where's it coming from?"

Tyrone smiled. "Good," he thought, "They're keeping their cool and the magic is protecting us."

The group pushed forward further and like a knife going through butter, they forced a passage amongst the crowd. People rose curiously but unhurt looking around for the cause. People assumed it was a wind hurling them over, as Tyrone smiled comfortably, with the truth disguised.

They got further along the street where the hospital came into view. There were still many cars and lorries parked ahead of them. Crowds stood all around, as far as they could see. People were both curious and naturally worried for the children in the hospital. The heroes saw flames coming from windows at the top of the hospital. They could hear anxious shouts from the crowds. They could also hear the distant sound of sirens from the fire engines and ambulances trying to get through to the scene.

The dinosaurs gasped at the scene. David craned his neck as high as he could.

"I know what's causing the blockage," he drawled. "There's a big traffic crash on that main road over there, on the main road. The cars have backed up with nowhere to go. All the people walking around have stopped to watch."

"Oh heavens," cried Tyrone, "We'll never get through and those poor children. We've got to do something pretty quick."

Shaun pondered hard as the seconds ticked by. Sweat poured from his brow. He had a solution.

"If the people see who you are, it might frighten them away and give us some room." The dinosaurs nodded.

Chloe and Trevor also had a plan. She whispered in his ear and suddenly they took off.

# Chapter 11

For an instant, Shaun thought that his little sister had become frightened and that she had asked Trevor to take her back. The dinosaurs wondered what Trevor was playing at. Shaun was about to contact Chloe when the little girl beat him to it. Shaun's mobile phone rang and he listened intently.

"Ho ho, good girl," he beamed. "Chloe and Trevor are going to fly straight up the head of the crowd and start to chase people away so we can push up from the back."

"Marvellous," Tyrone nodded enthusiastically. "Keep up with pushing the onlookers and stay calm so they won't see and get scared. Don't forget, they won't expect to see us as we are. They may be a nuisance, but we are here to protect them too."

The dinosaurs resumed their positions in pairs. The heaviest ones took the front to give the greatest pressure and the smaller ones followed up to support the initial thrust and to push back any people who tried to return.

Peter felt useless, travelling on David's back. Shaun noticed his glum expression every time the others put their might to the cause and he could not help.

"Peter, we need a lookout to watch for the emergency vehicles arriving. We're all facing one way and it would help for someone to watch our backs. We might miss them and the road could get blocked again," he said, reassuringly. Peter shuffled and turned his bulky frame around.

Peter grinned and Tyrone winked approvingly at Shaun. He admired his little pal's consideration when he recognised one of the team needed support.

Chloe and Trevor were high above with an excellent view of the scene ahead. Below, the group was steadily making its way through the onlookers. Few people resisted and many looked around dumbfounded as they were blown aside by an invisible force. Although the group was progressing, it was certain that the crowds would close over again.

If the emergency services could not arrive, the dinosaurs and their little human friends had a chance to rescue the children. Time was crucial. They had to act quickly.

The sirens grew louder. Everyone knew that the professionals were coming. Peter saw distant blue lights.

Although help was on its way for the children in the hospital, it still had to overcome the difficult traffic conditions.

The front of the crowd was about 100 yards from the hospital car park. It was flooded with anxious onlookers. Although they meant well, their presence and the traffic accident in town had simply blocked the way ahead for the emergency services to get through easily.

Tyrone rubbed his huge snout, looking for a solution. Shaun looked around anxiously assessing the scene and trying to locate a breakthrough.

Stanley, who had said little during the journey remarked suddenly,

"We've got to reveal who we are. We have to get through. It's useless relying on to our secret. We must mad, show ourselves and frighten these people away. We have to get to those kids!"

The group nodded as one.

Tyrone had never revealed his true self to grown-ups. He knew his moment was due. So did everyone.

"It is now or never," he roared. "Get angry everyone. Roar at everybody around you."

Shaun chuckled. This was naughty but he fancied some mischief. He contacted Chloe and told her details of the plan. The little girl chortled and reached forward to tell Trevor.

Trevor shrieked and winked at Chloe. The pair dive-bombed as quickly as they could. As they descended, they gave blood – curdling, high – pitched shrieks, louder than the loudest whistle and as fearsome as the loudest firecracker.

As they flew in hard towards the front of the crowd, Trevor's small eyes widened and Chloe's fair locks spread out fanning behind her little head.

They were a fearful sight, as Trevor had now lost his disguise. To the unsuspecting crowd, what sort of monster was this? Chloe's scream was so intense that people covered their ears.

As they saw the pair rapidly dropping upon them, the people in the front spun away quickly and pushed others aside.

The airborne duo dropped to within inches of the crowd. They soared upwards and dropped again. This time, people pushed harder against those behind them to flee the terror from the skies as a gap appeared.

Shaun saw this from his command position.

"Tyrone, we should push forward and sideways also. Chloe and Trevor have made an opening at the front. If we can make a breakthrough, we'll get control and keep a gap open for the fire engines."

"I hope so," whispered Tyrone.

"Push harder everyone," he urged.

The group took a breath and leapt forward. People turned away, aghast. They saw prehistoric monsters amongst them. Little did they know that these beasts were rescuers!

People broke away, though no one was hurt. The crowd panicked and moved together to give access to the heroes.

# Chapter 12

The brave band forced its way through the crowd and was close to the main entrance. Finally, they had an advantage. The issue now was how to use their strengths to help the children.

They paused. Chloe and Trevor hovered above assessing the aerial picture as Shaun looked around gauging the situation.

The sirens grew louder, but the vehicles were still a long way off.

Shaun saw flames coming from several windows on the ground floor. It was an old brick building. He figured that its supports would be strong and some materials wouldn't catch alight before they could attempt a rescue.

He remembered seeing fire doors that were heavy keep back flames. He considered that the hospital must have had some.

A fearful cry came from the roof. As they looked up, the group saw a tiny girl with a nurse waving frantically.

Before anyone could say anything, Trevor rushed upwards to the roof. Squawking to Chloe en route, she nodded and made ready.

The duo hovered alongside the railing on the roof. The nurse stared in amazement and froze. Chloe thrust out her arms towards the little girl and beckoned her. The little girl moved cautiously forward. As she reached the edge, Trevor carefully hovered, spreading one huge wing as a shield to disguise the drop below. The nurse realised what was happening and passed the little girl over.

Chloe grabbed her fiercely. Putting here phone into her pocket, she gripped the reins with one hand and held the frightened little patient with the other.

"Cheebo – da – tooli – dattu – neegy – dap," she barked to Trevor.

Trevor understood and glided to the ground so that the little girl would not fall.

People below gasped and cheered. They whistled in approval.

As they landed, an off-duty nurse rushed forward to comfort the little girl.

"Can you organise some help till the fire engines and ambulances arrive?" Shaun asked her.

"Of course," she replied. "Good luck to you. You're all very brave." She called for volunteers and asked for people to clear the way. People eagerly rushed forward to assist and the onlookers moved back to give valuable space to work in.

The sirens grew louder but the situation was hugely dangerous. The ambulances should have been there by now. There would be many sick children in their beds. The nurses would not leave them, so the problem was even greater.

Shaun observed the nurse on the roof. Others might follow her. If the fire blocked the way out, leaving the only route by the roof, Trevor could not lift everyone else off. They had to break through and find another means of escape.

"Come on gang, we've got to get inside and find ways out," he roared. The group rushed forward and reached the main doors of the hospital.

# Chapter 13

Chloe and Trevor knew where they were of best use. Trevor flew swiftly to the roof where another small child stood with the nurse. He hovered at to the roof's edge, as Chloe coaxed the little boy to join her.

He stopped, fearful and began to cry. The nurse reassured him as Chloe smiled sweetly.

"Ne – googo – lalap chagga," she whispered.

The little boy understood and cautiously put his leg over the side. Chloe gripped him firmly with her small but powerful hand and soon, Trevor glided gracefully to the ground below.

As they landed, several helpful onlookers rushed forward to take the little boy to safety at a first aid station that the off-duty nurse had organised.

Shaun pointed this out to Tyrone.

"They are useful doing that but what of the older children? I don't think either of them is strong enough to hold one to a bigger one.'

Tyrone nodded grimly.

"I agree, little chum. The emergency services haven't arrived yet; we could be up against the clock."

They looked quickly around for other ways to reach the roof. A ball of fire exploded through a window in the middle section of the hospital. The fire was strongest there and now there were two problems: people trapped above who could not be reached and there was a danger of the ceilings collapsing on those on the lower floors.

Trevor and Chloe soared to the roof again where a procession of frightened children gathered around the cool-headed nurse comforting them.

"Na – gaddad – oopattat – de – mapu," Chloe declared. Trevor nodded, knowing that they had a frantic task ahead of them. They could continue, lifting one child at a time but as bigger children appeared and they could not bear the weight.

Shaun rubbed his brow and shouted suddenly.

"Hey, have you all still got the rope you brought from the park?"

Everyone looked around and nodded.

"We must be quick. Let's see if we can put together a rope ladder. I reckon Trevor can fly to the roof. Chloe can attach one end to something and we can hold the other."

"Brilliant," Tyrone agreed, "Let's move it."

At once, every piece of rope was produced. There were different lengths, but it looked solid. The twins, Amy and Imelda stepped forward. They had the nimblest claws and rapidly started to tie the lengths together.

In minutes, the excited troupe created a splendid ladder with rungs that the older children could use to climb down to safety.

The group inspected their work as Shaun promptly announced, "We must rig it up at once. Time is running out."

He picked up his mobile phone and called Chloe. He waved to her and she immediately acknowledged the plan. She whispered in Trevor's ear and he dived quickly to the ground.

"CoCo, you must tie this end very tightly to something on the roof so the children can step over the side," he warned his little sister.

"Fapo – lee – lee – mag – igee," she chortled and Shaun was confident that she would do her best.

The bold aircrew took to the sky again. Trevor rose carefully so that Chloe would not drop the ladder and lose time in the rescue. As they reached the roof, Chloe pointed out the top of a drainpipe. Trevor hovered and Chloe pulled at the pipe to test its strength. It was firm.

She looped the end of the ladder over the pipe and with her deft little fingers, secured it firmly around the bolts holding it to the roof. She pulled on it and it held.

They looked down to check how far the ladder stretched. To their horror, they saw that it was short of the ground and wafted in the wind.

Shaun saw the problem too. "The children will fall off that and hurt themselves," he announced seriously. "It's too short after all and it's loose as well. What shall we do?"

David lumbered forward as fast as his heavy legs could carry him. He stood at the base of the wall. Using his great might, he pushed his front legs up the wall, stretched his long neck upwards and grabbed the ladder with his jaws and held it firmly.

"Look at the clever old thing," Tyrone shouted joyously. "There's nothing dozy about him when he means business!"

Seeing this, the nurse on the roof, beckoned an older child. She took his arms and gently told him what to do. She trusted him as one of the most helpful patients and he would be an example to the others.

The boy bravely went to the top of the ladder. He looked down and froze in fear. Chloe sensed this and prompted Trevor to go back to the rooftop. They soared upwards and Chloe waved to the nurse to bring forward a smaller child to transport.

The nurse brought forward a sleepy toddler and passed her over to Chloe. She whispered to Trevor to drop slightly and move outwards to give the older boy room. This would shield his view of the ground below and provide a cushion if he stumbled.

The boy, prompted by his nurse took a step over the edge. He turned to climb downwards. Chloe and Trevor remained close by as David kept a firm grip on the foot of the ladder. With confidence, the boy shouted,

"Let's go – no fear." He climbed down the rungs steadily and the aircrew followed at a safe distance. Within a short time, he reached the bottom. He was now unsure.

Shaun saw the problem and shouted swiftly, "Slip down David's neck onto his back. Think of him as a giant slide."

The boy slid along David's smooth skin. He passed along his neck, his broad back and onto his tail. David had curled his tail upwards so that the boy would not shoot off violently.

He came to a sudden stop as people cheered and rushed forward to comfort him.

"One down," Shaun mused, as he looked anxiously at the fire raging from the middle of the hospital. "We have to get to those children inside who can't leave their beds."

Chloe and Trevor flew again to the roof. With the nurse's help, they would keep ferrying the younger ones. The nurse would help the larger ones to climb over whilst David held the ladder. The fire had not yet reached their area so they could continue for the present.

Another fireball suddenly erupted in the centre of the building amid anxious gasps from the onlookers.

"No more time to lose," Shaun announced gravely, "We have to get inside and do something."

He jumped off Tyrone's back and ran to the doors on the ground floor. To his relief, nurses and doctors started coming out with patients, some in beds. Shaun assumed that they must have been on the ground floor, but others were still inside.

He saw a man in a set of overalls. He assumed he was a caretaker.

He grabbed the man's arm. "Can you tell me where that fire's coming from?"

The man replied nervously, "I'm sure, it's in the kitchen. It's none of the wards, though it may spread."

"Is anyone in the kitchen?" Shaun pressed him.

"The kitchen staff: the cook and five assistants."

Shaun knew that they could be seriously injured. The spreading fire would endanger everyone else in the whole building. They had to get in to rescue the grown-ups and the sick children too.

"It's grim, friends," he stated soulfully. "Let's do what we can."

Amy noticed a plume of smoke coming from the side of the ground floor. She grabbed Imelda and they raced off into the building by the automatic doors where the patients were still emerging.

"What are you doing?" Tyrone asked worriedly.

"We don't have the strength to lift people as the others can, but we can hold fire hoses and put out flames. We know the hospital must have some. We'll tackle the fire down here if you lot can do your bit!"

The twins suddenly responded, "That goes for us too. We can tackle the middle."

Valerie, feeling a little unemployed, sighed.

Shaun saw her dismay. "Valerie, all our work will be useless if the emergency services cannot get through. Look, the crowds are gathering again blocking the road. If we can't keep it free, they won't arrive."

Valerie agreed, "Yes, they won't like me chasing them away when I'm mean! Come on Steve and you, Stanley. You can be my backup squad. You can use muscle on them if they won't shift!"

The three friends faced the crowd. On Valerie's command, the larger beasts stood on her flanks and walked menacingly towards it. The people saw the angry group approaching and took to their heels leaving a gap in front of the hospital.

Not satisfied, Valerie delved deeper, forcing the bystanders further back. The main road was clear. Beaming, she yelled, "Don't anyone move forward. Let the ambulances and fire engines arrive safely and do their job. If anyone moves, my friends here will deal with you!"

Steve and Stanley walked slowly up each side of the main avenue like policemen on patrol. They scowled at the crowd. They knew that humans were curious creatures, so they thought it wise to keep vigilant until the police arrived.

The little group had restored some control. Valerie rushed to and from the hospital entrance, supervising the patients and staff that departed, ushering them to safe areas. She relished the responsibility.

The sirens grew louder. Help was close at hand. However, the fire had a hold on the building, as other plumes of smoke appeared. Amy and Imelda dashed straight into the ground floor and followed the smoke. Ducking to avoid breathing it in, they reached the stairs to the first floor where the smoke was thicker.

They crouched lower and noticed the fire hose in a glass cabinet on the wall. Amy turned. With a flick of her tail, she smashed the glass, as Imelda noticed flames that appeared on the ceiling. They drew the hose at once and Amy twisted the nozzle. A strong jet of water emerged, as they held the pipe firmly. Soon, they controlled it. Little by little, the flames died out, as they moved along the corridor.

After noticing that the flames had disappeared, Imelda opened some windows, let out the thick smoke. Quickly, they controlled the first floor. Many doors were already closed and offices were empty. No one was trapped and the smoke had not spread elsewhere.

Meanwhile, the twins entered from the rear and ran up the staircase towards the next floor. Here, the smoke was thick. Without hesitation, they rushed to the large glass windows in the lounge area. Using their heads, they broke the windows, releasing the smoke into the air outside. They carefully checked that there were no flames around to feed off the air.

Pamela popped her head inside the closed fire doors. A huge plume of black smoke passed over her head as she ducked and held her breath. It raced out into the lounge and vanished through a broken window.

"Is anyone in there?" she screamed. "Help me!" replied a croaky voice. She noticed a man lying on the floor some distance ahead waving his arm weakly. She saw fire behind the man in the centre of the corridor. It appeared to shoot out from a room to the left. The man had fallen and he had a nasty cut over his eye.

The twins looked at each other. Without a word, they dashed towards the man. Grabbing an arm each, they spun around and dragged him swiftly back towards the fire doors.

As they reached them, they barged them open with their heads and brought the man into the lounge, which was now full of fresh air, thanks to the broken window.

The man sat up, blinked and rubbed his eyes. "Am I seeing things?" he announced noticing the charming smiles on the twins' faces.

"No, we're real and so is this fire. You must follow us quickly to safety," Paul replied.

Lifting himself gingerly, the man held onto the twins' backs. As they raised him, his feet trailed. All three then trotted off to the staircase. Soon the twins delivered him to the ground.

Two men rushed forward from the crowd and gathered the man and took him over to the temporary first aid post where the off-duty nurse greeted them.

# Chapter 14

Chloe, Trevor and David continued their steady work of lifting children from the roof. But now, the fire had flared up again. An explosion appeared on the other side, probably where gas had been ignited. There were children trapped behind it.

Chloe and Trevor immediately flew to investigate but before they arrived, a young boy, stunned by the blast, lost his balance and toppled over the rear of the roof wall.

Trevor quickly followed hoping to catch him before he hit the ground. People at that spot saw what happened and screamed in fear. They closed their eyes, horrified.

At once, a squelching noise resounded. As Trevor descended, he saw that the boy had landed on Peter who was in the pond behind the hospital. No one had noticed Peter when they arrived. As his skin dried out, he went to find water to refresh himself. Luckily, he was swimming as the boy fell and he moved into position to cushion his fall.

The boy roared with glee when he stood up on Peter's back. The watching crowd clapped and cheered.

Peter gently swam to the edge and ushered the boy to dry land where he ran to another nurse who called him to safety.

Peter saw that other children were trapped and called out. "Don't be afraid, jump and I'll catch you."

A little girl timidly stood on the roof. She closed her eyes and jumped. Peter judged the angle of her fall and moved into position. He flipped onto his back and waited for her landing. He breathed deeply and extended his stomach like a large balloon. The little girl fell safely onto him.

"Come on children, one at a time. Think of it, like a ride in the fairground," Peter joked to the others on the roof.

The children gathered confidence and in an orderly fashion, lined up to jump off. An older boy made sure the younger ones went first and saved himself for last.

In a few minutes, eleven children jumped safely. The older boy took his turn and he stepped over the edge. He dropped at an awkward angle, as people below gasped. Peter quickly swam to the edge of the pond. He clambered out and rolled onto his back on the lawn. The boy fell wide of the pond. Peter took a quick breath and extended his stomach once more. The boy landed on him, knocking the wind out of him. The spectators applauded.

The sirens were louder. Soon, the professionals would be there. The children on the roof had all been rescued. The brave nurse stayed to the last and had slid down David's long neck and body. She felt like a schoolgirl at the fair. The flow of patients coming out with the staff had trickled away. The smaller dinosaurs felt they had contained the fires well. When the fire crews arrived, they could be certain. As far as everyone knew, all the children had been safely removed from the hospital. Shaun was uneasy about what had happened in the kitchen. Other people might have been seriously hurt. He remembered Mum saying how gas could explode very easily and he figured that this had happened.

He was not sure that everyone inside had been saved. He could not hold back hoping that the emergency services would arrive in time to rescue the people. He looked sadly at Tyrone.

"I know my little friend. I know what you're thinking. We can't stand by," he consoled.

Tyrone looked around. The smaller dinosaurs had all returned to the ground. The aircrew and David had wandered across and the outside dinosaurs were still guarding the crowd. Peter was enjoying the appreciation of his new friends at the rear.

"I think there are more people in the kitchen. We should go in from both sides," Shaun announced solemnly. "There are staircases at each end, but we can't take chances with the lifts, as we might get trapped. Too much weight stops them operating."

"We should go in in teams," Shaun added. "We have to be very quick and to look out for one another. The fire looks like it started in the middle. If the explosion stunned the people in the kitchen, they may be lying on the floor. If there is smoke, we've got to go in low."

The dinosaurs nodded. They quickly split into two teams. Shaun, Tyrone, Imelda, Amy and Stanley agreed to enter from the right as Valerie, the twins, Steve, Tricia and David chose the left. Shaun called to Chloe and Trevor to guard the building and look out for anyone else trying to escape on the roof. Peter saw the teams splitting and going inside. He returned to the pool in case anyone else leapt from the roof.

"We'd better take the rope with us," Imelda suggested. "It may come in useful."

"Good thinking," Tyrone replied. "It's best if we take some in each team."

David tugged at the ladder, bringing it to the ground. Tricia stepped forward and bit into the rope ladder, cutting it neatly down the middle to leave two strong ropes.

Imelda took one and passed the other to Valerie. The teams parted and ran to the staircases at each end of the ground floor. They had to reach the second floor quickly but safely. The smaller dinosaurs had quickly learned to use the handling fire hoses so they were ready for action. The bigger ones had the strength to move heavy objects and pull people away.

Both teams quickly reached the second floor. No patients were there as it was made up of offices, the kitchen and canteen areas. The visitors and office staff had evacuated when the alarms had sounded and had wisely closed the fire doors behind them trapping the fire and most of the thick, harmful smoke. However, no one realised that people were still inside the kitchen.

Tyrone looked through the glass on his side to see dense smoke in the air. David did likewise.

"I can't see anything," groaned Tyrone. "How can we search if we can't see where we're going?"

"There's nothing else for it," Shaun announced boldly. "I'll have to crawl in and take a look. I'm the smallest and I can crawl quickly along the floor. I know the smoke will rise so if I keep low, I shouldn't breathe it in."

Tyrone was aghast but knew that his little pal was right.

Valerie, the smallest dinosaur had the same idea. She knew she was the quickest and could do an inspection efficiently.

Amy considered the safety aspect. "Tie the rope around Shaun's waist. If he gets into difficulty, we can pull him out."

"Of course," Tyrone agreed, scolding himself for being so slow to think of this.

Quickly, Amy and Imelda deftly tied one end of the rope around Shaun's slender waist ensuring that the knot was secure. Valerie asked the twins to tether the other piece of rope around her.

Tyrone opened the fire door gently. The heat hit him, as he ducked. He realised that this was a massive danger to everyone. The smoke was still thick and deadly.

He pulled his little pal back before he could enter. "It's too dangerous Shaun. We can't fight this fire and rescue the people in there."

Valerie popped her head inside the door at the opposite end and realised the predicament.

The heroes who had been hopeful were now defeated. The firefighters were close, but time was vital.

Shaun had an idea.

"Tyrone, you haven't told me much about the Magician. If he is really powerful, wouldn't he help if we called him?"

Tyrone was stunned. He had never called on the Wizard and he was frightened of doing it.

The other dinosaurs looked at Tyrone. "We've got to try something," he answered slowly.

"What about the whistles?" Shaun added. "You said they were for emergencies. If you all blow as hard as you can, perhaps he will hear and come and help us?"

Tyrone had forgotten about the whistles during the frantic action.

"Everyone, get your whistle and blow. Wish for the Wizard to come to us," he urged.

Together, the group drew their whistles and blew mightily. Valerie heard the loud sound and instinctively recognised it was a danger call. She quickly shouted to the others to join them. The whistling increased, as the second party joined in.

Trevor heard the din and quickly cackled to Chloe to blow his. She reached forward, drew Trevor's whistle and blew with all her might.

Peter heard the sound and followed. As the dinosaurs had shown themselves, the magic had faded and the whistles were no longer silent to human ears. The noise deafened the crowds.

The brave rescuers held their breath and waited: nothing. An eternity seemed to pass, as each one heard their heartbeat sounding. Would the Wizard hear their call?

# Chapter 15

The group looked defeated. Shaun was about to charge in regardless when Tyrone grabbed his arm. Suddenly, a brilliant light shone in the sky. The spectators turned away to avoid being dazzled. Tyrone looked up in amazement. The whole group stood still in wonderment.

The landing lit up with a warm, white glow, as a deep, reassuring voice spoke.

"Go on my brave friends, do your duty!"

Tyrone and Valerie cautiously peered inside the fire doors. The fire and the smoke had vanished. The light lit up the kitchen where they saw six people lying on the floor. No one was burned but several had minor cuts. Everyone was unconscious.

The two groups raced inside from both ends. Fortune was with them for now but they had no idea how long the Magician's power would help them. They could not linger.

"Let's move it," Shaun bawled, as both teams ran towards each other.

The kitchen staff lay in the corridor. They must have fallen into the blast and been knocked out. Everyone had bumps or cuts on their heads. They were scattered apart so that the rescuers could remove them easily.

The cook was a big man with a long grey beard. Stanley and Tricia lumbered forwards and grabbed an arm each in their jaws. They dragged him back towards the fire doors. Amy kept the doors apart as he was taken to safety.

The twins reached the junior waitress and grabbed her arms. Together, they pulled away through the same door and lay her gently alongside the cook.

Imelda and Valerie grabbed the supervisor, a middle-aged lady and pulled her to safety in the same way.

Tyrone picked up the two other waitresses and placed them on Steve's back and Shaun held up their trailing legs. Steve ferried the waitresses to the safety point where Tyrone placed them also alongside their colleagues.

The last casualty was the deputy cook who was the most injured. His arm looked broken. Shaun remembered the first aid that his Grandma had shown him. He found a broom and asked Tyrone to break it. Gathering some cloths from the kitchen, Shaun made a splint and gently tied the pieces of wood to each side of the man's arm.

He asked David to lift the man. With Tyrone's help, they placed him carefully on Steve's back and walked slowly to the safety point where they lowered him.

Shaun looked at the unconscious casualties. They were all breathing. They would survive. They had reached them in time!

He turned to the rest dolefully. "We haven't got time to take these people to the ground. We must wait for the firefighters and paramedics to treat them. They are away from danger for now. The Wizard must have helped us by stopping the fire. Did you hear his voice?" Everyone agreed and blessed their good fortune.

"I don't know for sure if the fire has gone out. There may be gas leaking. We need to be sure or the rescuers will have problems."

Tyrone was fearful whether the magic would protect them. Had the Wizard completely removed the danger or was it temporary?

Shaun had to be certain. He had a keen sense of smell and would smell leaking gas immediately. He opened the fire door, looked around and sniffed the air. He detected a faint smell of gas. He opened the door wide behind him to allow in the fresh air and walked into the corridor. The smell of gas grew stronger. He reckoned it was inside the kitchen and trotted to the doorway. He saw the badly damaged oven and alongside it, a broken gas pipe sticking into the air, hissing. That was the danger!

"Tyrone, I've found it," he called. Before anyone moved, David sauntered forward and gently lifted Shaun aside with his head. He swung his giant frame sideways and pushed the gas pipe flat against the wall, squeezing it under his weight, capping off the escaping gas.

Shaun ran around turning off the gas taps on the oven and he opened the windows.

"Let's seal these doors and wait for the rescuers," he announced.

David followed him and they dashed out of the fire doors, closing them promptly.

The sirens could be heard outside the building. The two policemen, who Shaun had seen in the Park, arrived first and set about moving the crowd back. The people moved back easily.

The first fire engine arrived. The crew emerged immediately and ran to the side entrance. Another appliance with a turntable ladder followed in seconds. Behind, a fleet of ambulances and police cars rolled up.

The group looked back and sighed. There were still trails of smoke rising from the building for the firefighters to tackle. The paramedics were ready to deal with casualties.

The crowd below helped out assisting the doctors and nurses to push the bed-ridden children towards the ambulances and escorting those who could walk.

The fire chief ran up the staircase to the first floor. He directed two firefighters to check that floor. As he reached the second floor, he saw Shaun and the six injured people. There was no sign of the dinosaurs.

"Hello, son. What happened here?" he asked with a puzzled look on his face.

"Well, me and my friends here…" Shaun was about to tell the tale when he realised that the dinosaurs must have become invisible again and the fire chief couldn't see them. How could he tell him the truth?

He heard a faint chuckle behind him, as Tyrone briefly reappeared. Shaun knew his friends had not departed. He rubbed his tired eyes as they all reappeared. They put their fingers to their lips so that Shaun would not speak. He knew that as they had regained their calmness, they had returned to their usual state. The grown-ups couldn't see them as he could.

The fire chief smiled sympathetically. He assumed that Shaun had been a patient and that the ordeal had been too much for him. He didn't push him any further.

Within seconds, two more firefighters joined them and the chief ordered them to check the floor. Shortly, afterwards, four paramedics came to treat the injured.

Shaun told the chief paramedic what had happened. He looked puzzled and he tried not to laugh. He patted Shaun on the head and told him that he must have bumped his head and become confused. He smiled and played along with Shaun's wonderful tale.

He told Shaun to wait and one of his staff would deal with him as soon as the most injured people had to be treated. Shaun promised that he would stay, but he noticed Tyrone standing behind indicating with his eyes to make to the staircase.

As the paramedic tended to the deputy cook, Shaun slipped quickly to the head of the stairs, followed by Tyrone and the other dinosaurs in single file.

As they reached the bottom of the stairs, Chloe, Trevor and Peter were waiting. On the far side of the car park, they noticed an old man in a pointed hat and purple cloak. He had a kind face and gave them a broad smile from behind his bushy white beard.

"The Wizard," stuttered Tyrone, his lip trembling.

The group looked over in awe at the kindly figure. The wizard touched his lips and waved his wand. At once, the crowd and the noise disappeared. Everyone was covered in brilliant white cloud and everyone felt himself or herself being gently lifted into the air.

In seconds, they dropped gradually, as the cloud disappeared. They blinked and recognised that they were standing again in Dinosaur Park.

"Look, Shaun announced, there are Mum and Granddad Jim still looking at Tyrone's figure!"

The group laughed heartily and realised they were home after their brave adventure.

# Chapter 16

Tyrone scratched his snout as the other dinosaurs slapped each other on the backs and hugged.

"This baffles me, what did we do?"

"A very brave deed," replied a gentle, deep voice beside him.

As he turned, he saw the Wizard standing by. The dinosaurs bowed respectfully and Shaun began to follow.

"Stand tall, my friends," said the Wizard. "You have done well today in rescuing the children. You were all brave and thought only of saving others. I'm proud of you all," he continued joyfully.

"Sir, did you help us by stopping the fire?" Shaun asked quietly.

"Yes, I did. As you and Chloe are humans, I couldn't allow any danger to happen to you. You would have willingly risked your safety to help others. You showed your faith in the magic by deciding to call on me. The dinosaurs would not have found their bravery but for you two.

"Hurray," Tyrone shouted, "We need a party!"

"I think two worthy little people have had enough excitement for one day," the Wizard replied kindly. Perhaps, another day?

At that, the dinosaurs began to fade. Shaun knew that they had to return to their shells. He heard Mum and Granddad Jim talking and he realised that he and Chloe had returned to normal.

Suddenly, Shaun felt his body being lifted as Granddad Jim's face appeared in front of him.

"Hello sleepyhead. We're home now."

Shaun shook his head. He saw his garden and a bike. He saw Tassie waiting to greet him. He looked aside and saw Chloe in her little seat. Mum was getting out of the car.

He blinked and realised he had been asleep. The big adventure had been a dream, though it was so real. He felt disappointed. It had been lovely making friends with the dinosaurs and now, it was just in his head. He had been proud of his and his sister's bravery, yet it was simply make-believe.

He felt exhausted and wasn't hungry. He would fall into a deep sleep. As he put on his pyjamas, alone in his room, he looked at his 'T' Rex model. He took it gently in his arms. In his thoughts, he spoke to it.

"I wish it had all been real, Tyrone."

As he replaced the model on the cabinet, a whisper came from the model's mouth.

"It is Shaun, believe in the magic. When people need us again, we will come to the rescue and that includes you and Chloe!"

Shaun thought that his mind was playing tricks but he was too weary to concentrate. He was heartened by the voice. As his head touched the pillow, he went off into peaceful sleep, as Tyrone's voice gently called, "Sweet dreams my brave little friend!"

# Chapter 17

Shaun arose early the following morning, refreshed but confused about his dream. He had heard Tyrone's voice again before bedtime and this had baffled him. Was he imagining things?

As he came downstairs, he carried his T – Rex Model. When Chloe saw it, she waved enthusiastically at it and gabbled in greeting.

"She recognises it. How odd. She's chatting away to it," he thought.

He was worried about this dream more than any other. This one had been real…

As he put his coat on to go to school, he asked his Mum politely, "If Chloe and I are good this week, do you think that Granddad would take us back to see the dinosaurs again? I enjoyed that day out and I think Chloe did too," he added purposefully.

Shaun knew in his mind that he had to go back to confirm if his adventure had been his active imagination playing tricks on him.

Shaun vowed that when he grew up, he would do something really useful.

He went to school pondering on his adventure. His Mum noticed the unusual silence as he ambled along. He was lost in his world, thinking deeply about the great rescue.

Shaun went into class and when the teacher asked the pupils where they had been over the summer holidays, he was delighted to tell everybody about the huge model dinosaurs that lived in the Park.

He amazed everyone with a detailed description of all the dinosaurs and where they were inside the Park. He told class useful facts, like the size of the dinosaurs and what they ate.

By the end, they clapped and his teacher said, "I bet you wish they had been real Shaun, you could have had some adventures, couldn't you?"

"Yes, Miss," Shaun replied with a sigh, still haunted by his dream.

The day passed swiftly. Shaun got home and changed into his casual clothes. He looked at his T-Rex model. "I hope Granddad will bring us back to the Park. I need to be sure," he whispered.

That evening, Shaun met Granddad Jim at the gate and asked him sweetly if they could see the dinosaurs once more. Granddad said that provided that he and Chloe helped Mum, he would treat them to another visit that weekend. If Granddad said he would take them back to the Park, he would keep his word.

He went to bed and soon drifted off into a restful sleep. The hours passed quickly to the following morning.

For the rest of the week, Shaun was on his best behaviour. He told Chloe what Granddad had promised and she too was well behaved. They both helped Mum with little jobs like feeding the dog or taking the rubbish out.

Shaun made sure his bedroom stayed tidy and helped Chloe to look after hers. He desperately wanted to go back to the Park.

# Chapter 18

Granddad called one morning as they were still having breakfast.

"We'll have to make an early start. There will be lots of cars on the road. We don't want to be stuck in a traffic jam, do we?" he announced.

"Where are we going, Granddad?" Shaun enquired quietly though hoping that Granddad had not changed his mind.

"Where do you think, kids?" Granddad replied with a little knowing smile on his lips.

"Dinosaur Park!" Shaun shouted.

"Dee – do parka!" Chloe added as they all laughed, hearing her trying to copy Shaun.

"Coats on then – wrap uptight, it's a bit chilly," said Mum. Soon, they were in the car and ready to leave.

Shaun brought his T – Rex Model and Chloe carried a model of a Pterodactyl to remind them both of their special dinosaur friends who were waiting for them in the Park.

They drove along the familiar route, passing the docks and into the road tunnel and soon along the motorway. The weather was fine and the early morning dew disappeared, as the sun grew stronger.

They drove past the beach and the castle on the mountainside and along the expressway to the town where the Dinosaur Park lay. They got there quicker today. Granddad had predicted that the traffic would be heavier later and the earlier start had ensured that the roads would be free.

This was going to be a beautiful day – Shaun knew it as he looked happily at Chloe who returned his smile. She too was looking forward to the reunion.

Within minutes, Granddad drove off the main road into the slip road for the Park. Shaun knew the way and remembered that the entrance to the Park would only be a short walk across the grass, past the boating lake and then, paying the lady on the gate.

They parked up and got out. Shaun felt the excitement welling up within him. He helped Mum to secure Chloe in her buggy and winked at his little sister.

"Soon, CoCo," he whispered.

Everything was as familiar as the last visit, as they walked over the grass towards the entrance. Shaun spied the huge head of the T – Rex Model peering through the bushes.

In no time, Granddad paid for them to enter and Shaun knew exactly where to start.

"I want to see T- Rex first," he announced deliberately and trotted ahead of the group.

"Don't get lost," Granddad called after him, though it would have been difficult, as the paths were well marked. They would have met up again quickly.

Shaun raced up to the T-rex model, stopped and looked at it squarely. Quietly, he spoke to it.

"Tyrone, I know you can hear me. Did I just dream or was it something special?"

The rest of the family arrived and stood alongside him.

"You like this fellow the best, don't you?" Granddad asked studying the impressive monster. "I bet you'd like to have him in your garden."

Shaun watched, but nothing happened. He felt that he was talking to himself. He turned away downcast to follow his family to the next exhibit when a rustling sound distracted him.

He turned back to see the monster's head move slowly towards him. "Where do you think you're going?" it boomed in Tyrone's familiar voice. Shaun blinked nervously, looked back at his folks who suspected nothing and returned his glance to Tyrone.

"Yes, little pal, good old magic! We can see each other again but the grown-ups can't. Remember, time for them is frozen whilst we come alive and you can see us. Get Chloe and join us, we've something for you."

Shaun was reeling. This was no daydream.

He followed his folks and came up behind. He went to Chloe and noticed that Mum and Granddad were busy watching the next exhibit. He quickly unfastened Chloe's harness on her buggy and took her tiny hand and ran back to Tyrone's position. As he looked back, he was amazed to see a copy of him and Chloe standing with his Mum and Granddad.

"Magic, they think we're still there!" he reassured himself, joyfully.

He looked ahead where Tyrone beckoned them to join him. As they reached the corner, Tyrone waved them across.

In the middle of the Park, all their dinosaur friends had gathered and at the side, there was a huge table full of goodies for a party. Shaun's eyes marvelled at the fancy cakes and pastries and Chloe's little face beamed like the moon when she saw her favourite jelly.

The children shrieked with glee on meeting all their friends once more. Chloe ran up to Trevor and gave him a big hug and a kiss on his beak. Shaun ran and hugged Tyrone. The other dinosaurs came up in procession to earn their hugs.

Everyone was excited. It was just like the start of the great adventure all over again!

"What's the party for?" Shaun asked innocently.

"It's David's birthday today. This is a very special party," Tyrone replied as he nodded slightly to someone standing at the rear.

The children turned and recognised the Wizard standing quietly behind the group. The brilliant light no longer surrounded him and he looked just like a kindly Granddad. He had long white hair and a beard. He wore a velvet cloak draped over a shirt that was deep blue with stars and moons on it. His trousers were dark with sequins on.

He was old but his face was young. His deep blue eyes were full of kindness and laughter.

"Hello, children," he announced in a strong, calming voice. "We've been waiting for you to join us."

Shaun looked at him and Chloe chortled at his fancy cloak. The Wizard guessed that Shaun was unsure of what he was witnessing. Before Shaun could ask any questions, the Wizard spoke.

"I know you're confused. You're wondering if this is just a dream, but it isn't," he explained patiently. "You truly had a great adventure with the dinosaurs. The magic made you forget it right away."

"I don't understand. Why did it only come back in my dream?" Shaun asked curiously.

The Wizard continued. "You and Chloe proved your worth in the rescue. I couldn't let you remember the adventure straight away until I was certain that you would keep the secret of the magic. That's why we sent the dream. We send a dream first to give special children a choice. They can enjoy it as a wonderful memory or if they truly want to help, they seek to know more, as you did."

"We would keep the secret because we know it's important," Shaun added. "Chloe and I would never tell," he replied truthfully.

"I know that now," the Magician responded. "When you had your dream, you thought about it every day afterwards. That told me that you had a conscience and that I could trust you."

"So we *did* help the sick children and the injured grown-ups in the hospital?" Shaun asked with a huge smile. Chloe clapped her hands.

"Of course," the Wizard replied, graciously. Chloe had the same dream though she too didn't know it.

"What a surprise!" Shaun added turning towards his little sister.

The Wizard spoke again. "My dinosaurs did their part bravely. They were waiting for the chance. You children gave them the strength. The magic helped where it could, but it couldn't have worked without your courage."

Humans have done some silly things in their time but many good people want to make the world a better place. They care about others and you children showed your best when you risked your safety.'

Tyrone looked with proud tears in his eyes. Trevor rubbed his head along Chloe's cheek to praise her.

"Come here, my little ones. I have something for you," the Wizard added.

From under his cloak, he produced a silver box that he opened. Inside, two small, silver whistles shone in the sunlight.

"These are special whistles," he explained. "If you use them in your time of need, the dinosaurs will hear them and come to help you. The magic will protect you all again."

As the children stepped forward, the Wizard placed them around their necks.

"I thank my little friends for their great service. They are honest children with kind souls. May the Magic protect them!" The dinosaurs cheered.

"Thank you, Sir," Shaun replied humbly.

"Kee – doo – mip – na – gee – goo," Chloe replied gratefully.

"You are welcome,' the Wizard replied with a gentle bow. The dinosaurs all followed and bowed politely.

"What should I tell everyone if they ask me about our whistles?" Shaun asked nervously.

The Wizard laughed. "The magic will disguise the whistles. Only you and Chloe will know you are wearing them. They are yours alone to use if you are in need. Remember children, we may need you again."

Shaun smiled and Chloe gurgled with joy. The dinosaurs all rushed forward to congratulate them.

"Come now, you must be hungry. This food looks divine," the Wizard announced licking his lips.

"Pizza's mine!" Tyrone bawled revealing this favourite weakness.

"Sir, I don't know what to call you," Shaun asked quizzically.

"Well," the Wizard replied stroking his beard, "People call me various names, what do you suggest?"

"Middu – ba – rown," Chloe quipped before anyone else reacted.

"I think she said 'Mr Brown'," Shaun repeated.

"Mr Brown, I shall be then." The Wizard laughed heartily as everyone joined him.

At once, the group tucked into the tempting food on the table until they were soon full.

Time sped by when at last the Wizard held out his arms.

"We must go now," he announced as a sad look appeared on the children's faces. "Don't fret. We will always be here waiting for the call to duty," he added.

Tyrone nodded in agreement as the other dinosaurs nodded in confirmation.

"The dinosaurs will always live in this Park, children, so you know where to find them," the Wizard added in a kindly whisper.

As the children looked downcast, the dinosaurs lined up for a hug. Tyrone led the procession. "Don't be sad, my little pals. You know we are always here waiting for you. We will have another adventure soon, I'm sure of it," he added softly.

"You're right, you have to return to keep the magic secret," Shaun answered realising the situation. "See you all soon, eh?"

One by one, the dinosaurs stood and waved until the magic made them fade from view and return inside the models around the Park. The Wizard stood quietly until the last one had disappeared.

"Remember, children, keep the secret and think all the time of the dinosaurs. They will hear you and when you need each other, you will know."

He too began to fade as he waved to the children.

"Goodbye Mr Brown," Shaun whispered.

"Goodbye children. I do like that name," the Wizard replied, as he blew a kiss to Chloe. "Catch up with the grown-ups, there's plenty more for you to do today."

# Chapter 19

Shaun and Chloe saw that they were back with Mum and Granddad staring at the models.

"Come on then, are we going to look around?" Granddad asked.

The children kept quiet as the group wandered around the remaining models. As they passed each, a faint chuckle came out. The children knew that their friends were safely hidden from view and were watching them as they walked around.

About an hour later, the family walked to the shop to look at the gifts.

As they entered, Shaun saw the two policemen from his dream. They were chatting with the lady behind the counter.

"Yes, it's a complete mystery," one of them said, shaking his head doubtfully. "All the children and the hospital staff were evacuated and not one person was seriously injured. You know the patients must have suffered from some kind of delusion because when we got there, they were talking about two children and a gang of dinosaurs running around rescuing them! The daft thing is, people in the crowd agreed with them! What's more, doctors and nurses swore they had seen monsters running about – the fire must have damaged the anaesthetic gases and everyone must have been dreaming! The news people can't explain it either!"

Shaun put his hand over his mouth and turned to Chloe.

"It must be true, Co-Co. How could that policeman know unless he was there?"

Granddad heard the conversation and turned to Mum, shaking his head "Some people say the daftest things, policemen of all of them!"

"They certainly do," Shaun chortled under his breath. He turned his head away towards his little sister. The children chuckled silently, alone with their very special secret.

CPSIA information can be obtained
at www.ICGtesting.com
Printed in the USA
LVHW011200131221
706035LV00010B/744